The Twenty-One Irreverent Truths of Life

Amadeus

BALBOA.
PRESS

A DIVISION OF HAY HOUSE

Author photo credit: Craig Stuart

Balboa Press books may be ordered through booksellers or by contacting:

Balboa Press
A Division of Hay House
1663 Liberty Drive
Bloomington, IN 47403
www.balboapress.com
1 (877) 407-4847

Because of the dynamic nature of the Internet, any web addresses or
links contained in this book may have changed since publication and
may no longer be valid. The views expressed in this work are solely those
of the author and do not necessarily reflect the views of the publisher,
and the publisher hereby disclaims any responsibility for them.

The author of this book does not dispense medical advice or prescribe the use
of any technique as a form of treatment for physical, emotional, or medical
problems without the advice of a physician, either directly or indirectly. The
intent of the author is only to offer information of a general nature to help you
in your quest for emotional and spiritual well-being. In the event you use any
of the information in this book for yourself, which is your constitutional right,
the author and the publisher assume no responsibility for your actions.

Any people depicted in stock imagery provided by Thinkstock are models,
and such images are being used for illustrative purposes only.
Certain stock imagery © Thinkstock.

Printed in the United States of America.

ISBN: 978-1-4525-8534-5 (sc)
ISBN: 978-1-4525-8536-9 (hc)
ISBN: 978-1-4525-8535-2 (e)

Library of Congress Control Number: 2013919468

Balboa Press rev. date: 11/8/2013

Contents

Acknowledgments

To every happy moment and to every hurt experienced, I say thank you. There, I have satisfied karma. Now let me thank the good hearts who shared time and input to make *The Twenty-One Irreverent Truths of Life* a reality.

Bill Barns, good friend and very talented musician, thank you for the input on songs selected for each chapter. I learned a little bit about my own writings from the material you chose.

Josh Weber, wine connoisseur and the chosen one of cheese selections, I say thank you. Your words of support (and wise wine dedications) have meant a great deal to me.

And truly, in this case, the last shall be first. My beautiful wife, Lanna, endured many years of my fits and starts as I accumulated the bruises that have led to this diatribe of humor and philosophy. Thank you for being the patient soul who is always there with such a gentle and loving touch.

Truths is dedicated to Yona, my best fur-covered friend, who left my side July 1, 2013. The cover art work is a Spirit totem painting of Yona by artist extraordinaire Sioux Storm. Understanding who Yona's Spirit guides in this life were brought the two of us closer as fellow travelers on the same plane. Thank you Sioux for sharing your special gifts and thank you Creator for placing all of these wonderful beings on the same playground at the same time with me.

Much love to all!

Prologue

T he *Twenty-One Irreverent Truths of Life* is intended for those who like to laugh as they pursue a course in the basic building blocks of how to take life head-on.

There are only three topics of discussion in which we ever engage. The first is people. We spend a lot of time digging into other people's motives, peculiarities, and blunders. Humans normally look out across the landscape, and the first items they see are people, and that is what generates the basis of our conversations.

Certainly when we discuss the beauty and wonderments of our own individual endowments, we are still on the plane of talking about people. For the most part, our opinions of others (and ourselves) are based on emotion, with varying degrees of objectivity. Gossip resides at one end of the scale and empirical performance reviews lie at the other. Either way, we are talking about people.

Second comes the topic of things. Things are physical manifestations that can be red, shiny, fast, green, soft, or sweet smelling. Things can delight us, serve us, or make us frightfully agitated. In any case, things (for the most part) do not meet the standard of anything found beyond three-dimensional boundaries.

Things can be quite wonderful, and without things we would certainly perish. Banish the thought of banishing things! Understand them for what they are, and credit to them the due they deserve.

Third, we occasionally stray into the arena of ideas. People and things exist in a reality that isn't real, while ideas and the spirit of being live in a surreal amphitheater in which we are fearful to tread.

Ideas start as seeds and can grow into magnificent comprehensions of infinite capacity. We place the limitations on ourselves, because ideas are amorphous and seem to have no quantifiable essence.

If you can craft a germ of an idea within a group while feeding the idea with dialogue, it will allow the thought to take on a gestalt and allow the genuine participation of human cognition.

Elevating discourse from people and things to the arena of ideas opens the door to better understandings and, prayerfully, more love. The easier it is to don the mantle of higher thought, the easier it is to share thoughts and esoteric values.

On the surface, this book appears to be trite and overly simplistic, and in a way that is exactly what it is. The concept behind it is to open minds and hearts in the arena of ideas by serving as a starting point for discussion.

Each chapter is about four pages long for a reason. The intent is not to beat some philosophical treatise into someone's head. If you read a chapter in a group, consider having the reader begin a discussion on the idea laid out on the four pages.

Every chapter is paired with a suggested wine, cheese, and song with a tie to the theme of that particular chapter. Read the chapter, drink the wine, slice the cheese, and listen to the song on whatever service you use for music.

This process lends itself quite handily to a small group of friends. All the book does is place the participants at a starting point. The written words are not a boundary. Wherever you and/or your group go lends to the excitement and fun.

At the end of the adventure, there may have been some healing, some driving thoughts, and some small idea you can take home as your own. Nurture your idea, let it grow, and be amazed at how wonderful and real the surreal truly is.

Amadeus

Irreverent Truth of Life

Number 1

The Meaning of Life

How difficult can it be ascertaining the *meaning of life?* Monks, priests, theologians, philosophers, and the like have spent their lives poring over old manuscripts or in deep, Himalaya-induced meditations.

I am a busy guy, and I don't have a whole lot of time to spend on such matters. So I subbed out the *meaning of life* to some old friends of mine: Fido, Ralphie, and Fi Fi. Yes, they are dogs, but their consulting fees are quite reasonable.

Fido is a medium-sized, Benji-looking dog that is getting a bit long in the tooth. He lives here in the neighborhood and has just about seen it all. I guess if I were to characterize him, I'd say he's quiet, observant, and always first in line whenever there is a free handout to be had. He's a pretty sharp fella all the way around.

Ralphie is a big, fluffy English sheepdog yearling. To see Ralphie is to see nothing but happy, eager, and ready to discover. He looks up to Fido with a respect that dates back to another time.

Fi Fi was born with the looks. She is a French poodle with all the trimmings and bows. Most folks never get past the pretty, because they don't want to. Her family history includes aristocratic bloodlines, but her true ancestral purpose was to protect and to hunt. It's funny how a bouffant and pink ribbon disguises what lives between the pages.

It was a bright and sunny morning when Ralphie approached Fido with his big question of the day.

"Hey, Fido, hey uh, can you, uh, tell me the *meaning of life?*"

"Nope," deadpans Fido.

"Well, why not? I gotta know the *meaning of life.*"

"Can't tell ya, Ralphie. Won't do you any good. Tell you what though, if you follow me around today, maybe you'll learn the *meaning of life.* Ready?"

Fido takes off with Ralphie in tow. Pretty soon Fido finds a trash can full of loot. Over it goes, and right on top is a meaty T-bone. Fido lies in the sun and enjoys his well-found feast.

Once the T-bone disappears, Fido turns to Ralphie and asks, "How are you doing on that *meaning of life* thing? Got a handle on it?"

"Uh, no I really don't."

"Harumph. Well, keep following." And off they went.

That afternoon they spot Fi Fi in the meadow, and she's looking good.

"Ralphie, stay put. I'll be back later."

"Okay, Fido. I'll be right here."

Fido and Fi Fi spend the rest of the afternoon frolicking in the field. Fido returns to Ralphie, who is waiting patiently by the field. "Well, young dog, have you made any progress on this quest for the *meaning of life?*"

"No, sir, not yet, but I'm not giving up."

"We have one more stop. Keep following."

Two blocks away is the mayor's house, and in the driveway is a shiny, brand-new, fresh-from-the-showroom Mercedes-Benz convertible. Fido spots the new set of wheels and sniffs each tire. After his initial perusal, he hikes his leg and delivers a wetting blow to each of the four tires.

Fido returns to Ralphie. Ralphie says, "Wow great work there, boss."

"Yeah, got 'em all good. Tell me, son, after all that you have seen today, do you now know the *meaning of life?*"

"Oh, yes sir, I got it."

"Well, out with it, son."

"The *meaning of life* is, if it doesn't give you sustenance or love, then piss on it."

Song: "All You Need Is Love" by The Beatles

Wine: J. Lohr Cabernet Sauvignon

Cheese: Canadian Sharp

Irreverent Truth of Life

Number 2

If You Can't Drive in Your Own Lane...

This chapter was conceived around the Fourth of July or, more correctly, Independence Day. There are lessons, both large and small, that we can apply from America's founding document, the Declaration of Independence.

The concept (and practice) of free thought, private property rights, and individual free will are the attributes of a grounded individual and of a society that celebrates individualism. Using these ideals as a daily measuring stick in our interactions with one another gives a moral clarity that allows not only for sharing thoughts, but also for employing the respect that should be given to another's pursuits.

In our daily world, we occasionally encounter an errant driver who unintentionally wanders into our lane of traffic. And I will be the first to say that I have been guilty of such a transgression against my fellow traveler. Fortunately, I have never had a mishap, but the metaphor that speaks to the care we should give to our fellow travelers on this earth is readily available for thought and discussion.

Our natural rights, as endowed by our Creator, give us standing in this world in our pursuits. However, there is no written celestial order, sans the biblical philosophy of free will, that compels any of us to industry. We make our choices on how we wish to participate in life's endeavors, both good and bad, learn from those experiences, and then move on down the road.

When a learning experience occurs, we should look only unto ourselves as the author of such activity. To attach the outcome of our individual decision to another is the folly of an immature interpretation of reality and will serve only an internal master of self-deception. To project our failures on another is an act of forcefully traveling into our neighbor's space.

This isn't to say that concealment of error is always the best standard. Sharing a difficulty with another, while at the same time taking ownership of the problem, allows for the giving and receiving of care and, if needed, direction.

If an application of personal aptitude and/or effort results in abundance, humility should be your demeanor. An attitude of self-aggrandizement is purchased at the expense of your neighbors' leave, resulting in the obstruction of their path with your ego.

Original thoughts and ideas that come to us belong to us. Society has crafted protections for intellectual property that is generated by the individual. Yet, if we feel so motivated as to share the idea or invention, we lose ownership of it. There is a fine line between ownership of a social gift and the bequeathing of said item to your neighbors. Provided that you wish to be compensated for your effort of gift to society, then that falls within the natural laws of man that motivate industry and thought.

It is a perilous path a society follows that chooses to take from individuals without just reward and hence punish the universal class of industry by disallowing incentive. A guarantee of equal station and equal outcome creates a permanent dam in an individual's lane and thus stymies the free flow of traffic to the point of apathy and malignant lethargy.

To dream is to travel in an unfettered and surreal world of infinite possibilities and unlimited potentials. It is this world of openness to the cosmos and the whispers of our Creator that give rise to natural law and its earthly employment.

The most dastardly impediment placed in our path is the notion that free travel rests on the back of material acquisition. Our social contract with one another should revolve around ideas and the free association of thought and encouragement. When society defines success as physical manifestations of wealth, we have collectively driven into one another's lanes with the intent to demean the dreamer and the idealist.

We will all travel more freely on a highway woven with the thread of equal access for opportunity to seek excellence (or not). There are occasions that we seek fellow travelers on the same path, and that is a good thing. Understanding that we are individuals banded together still allows for personal application and individual input. To this specific end, one can properly draw the conclusion that the whole is greater than the sum of its parts.

And finally, for those of us who wish to travel in another's lane, please be so kind as to stay the hell out of mine.

Song: "Roam" by The B-52s

Wine: First Drop Mother's Ruin Cabernet Sauvignon

Cheese: Aged Gouda

Irreverent Truth of Life

Number 3

Buddha Lives in a Dog's Smile

How happy the moment is when we open the door and our good buddy, the Dog, is there waiting on our arrival. Is the tail an instrument of the dog, or is it vice versa? That doesn't really matter, because the wiggling and the uncontrolled joyful greeting is a delight we all live for. It is a fun moment, but it isn't the existential moment of teaching of which we shall speak.

The Buddha's teachings are based on acceptance of the world as it is. There are special moments when our best friend sits calmly with a knowing smile and just stares into space. The relaxed smile gives a feeling of a truly sated spirit with no other deliberation than existing in this time and space with no past or future considerations.

Our Creator is ever present and will place markers in our daily path to remind us that His actions are truth and can be found if we choose to look for them.

This exercise is best contemplated in the evening when all is quiet and the day's activities have settled.

To begin, we will note that the dog is balanced and in a meditative state. We might wonder as to what he may be thinking, but then we would be missing his point. The dog is not thinking. He is being. In a state of being there is no craving for sensuality, no need to acquire some self-aggrandizing special identity, no fear of annihilation, and no sadness that suffering is universal.

Is this reading a bit much into a dog's smile, or are we just harvesting a reminder of truths taught by the Buddha? Perhaps it's a starting point for us to think about just being and to allow our mind to wander. Can the sun and the moon be hidden? And if they cannot be hidden, then what about truth? Where do celestial truths end, and where is the beginning point of manmade boundaries that cast definitions with the intent to restrict free thought?

In our dog's world, there is no desire to ascend to a higher consciousness. For him, just being is enough. And in this state he understands that the way is not in the sky; the way is in the heart.

Looking a little deeper into our friend's eyes, we begin to survey the steps in a right path of view, intention, speech, action, livelihood, effort, mindfulness, and concentration. By contemplating these eight points (the Buddhist eight-fold path), are we setting ourselves up for a life change that removes doubt? Are we engaging in a fantasy here, or is this when we begin to awaken?

Monsoon season brings a cascade of fearful experiences to, Bella, our rescued schnauzer. She is consumed by a terrible and inconsolable fright during the thunder and rain, and all of her suffering is borne from a dreadful past prior to her finding sanctuary with us. No matter how we try to protect her, the old fears manifest in a trembling pain that is hurtful to watch.

We try to explain that it is all in her mind and that it will soon pass. Perhaps she could relay the same consoling words to us when we have moments of doubt and pain. The mind does indeed create suffering, and we allow it to do so because we have not learned how to decouple the pieces that build that anxiety.

The storm brings moments of doubt. And doubts build on themselves because they can be comforting as a crutch. Fear, loathing, and distrust mount as a poison that disintegrates all in its path. For our schnauzer, the doubts disappear with the sunshine. We, on the other hand, nurse our newfound blight and choose not to allow the sun to penetrate our shell. The difficulty we face is failing to conquer ourselves by generating an internal sunlight.

Perhaps the battle for our own heart is where mastery of our destiny derives. Maybe what our schnauzer needs is an example of truth and light and not just words. And truthfully, isn't our greatest aspiration, as well as our greatest struggle, trying to be the person our dog thinks we are? Perhaps that reflection of the Buddha in our friend's eye is really our soul looking for us?

The intent here is not to send someone off on a path of austere stoicism or to live as an ascetic. Again, let's look to our friend; we will see unbridled joy, love, and a desire to pursue happiness. If these things are working for him, let's take them and build upon his gift as the sentient beings we are.

Song: "My Back Pages" by The Byrds

Wine: Chateau St. Michelle Merlot

Cheese: Pecorino Romano

Irreverent Truth of Life

Number 4

Don't Bark if You Won't Bite

To take a bite out of something (or someone) requires teeth. That's pretty obvious once you think about it, but the clamping down of mandibles, metaphorically speaking, happens in only one of two ways. First is the visceral reaction that happens in a moment, usually without a warning bark, and the second is the occurrence after a timeline of events with some degree of barking attached.

Barking in and of itself is an art form. And within the world of art there are the untalented hacks that choose to use a single color and broad brush, and there are others who engage a palette so diverse that their message is lost in the abstract. And then there are those who articulate clearly and concisely.

Conveying a thought in the arena of ideas persuasively and with passion commands an understanding of facts, reality, and language. To bark a simple-minded talking point has no originality and garners only the support of those who paint with a single filament in a base pastel. Sadly, there is a plurality of the cognitively unengaged who enjoy barking just to be part of a pack that knows not of which they bark.

Joining the pack of cerebrally challenged canines are the dogs that bark for the mean sport of it. Some of the motivating factors here include baseless hatred, bias, bigotry, fear, envy, and a desire to be part of the gang that supports a mutt mentality of superiority over their intended target. The leaders of this horde of hounds are vile purveyors of pernicious malice designed to maintain a feckless frenzy that allows them to remain in control. The more threatened a cowardly cur feels, the louder and longer he or she will bark. Curiously, there is a surreal value attached to this category of noisemakers, and that value is credibility. These dogs can deliver a rabid bite, and becoming entangled in their murky ring rarely allows for a winning escape.

Obtuse barking has so many colors and variations that the majesty of delivery becomes the message. How can one discard a dialectic delivered in perfect pitch and harmony? A well-turned phrase of an idea in poetic structure soars in the mind of the receiver, and never is the question raised of fact or truth in relation to the orator's speech. The hypnotic beauty of ungrounded existentialism leads the listeners into a realm where they no longer wish to bite, and their granted wish rests on logic that has no basis in reality.

To bark rationally, logically, and with an educated viewpoint places one squarely in the arena of ideas. Bark with passion, yet bark with respect of the other dog's viewpoint. This isn't to say that you should surrender your core values to another; it is more to say that persuading hearts and minds is the order of the day.

There will come a time when you must decide whether your ideas and convictions are worth standing for. If you decide not to prosecute your ideas to their fullest, sit down and stop yapping. We have enough pit-yorkies in the world.

We know about those who bark for no purpose other than to serve their masters or their immaterial, cloud induced air-headed selves. They are in the arena, and despite the fact that they have more negative to offer, that should not cause you to lie down and play dead.

If you choose to walk on your hind legs, then do so. A question was once asked regarding life and peace being so dear that the price of chains and bondage would be a reasonable sacrifice. To bite is the final act of those who have no other answer.

The question for any engaged individual is at what point do I surrender or take up fangs to defend myself, family, and/or neighbors? History is filled with instances where barking continued long after the time when a good bite should have been delivered. Unfortunately, there are many occasions where bites were prematurely inflicted when there was still plenty to bark about, which eventually would have ended in peace.

If you wish not to bark in a thoughtful, honest, and fully informed way, please stay on the porch. Too often it is your type that throws the first bite. And to those who have no woof (resonance) to their bark, stay under the porch. We really don't need anyone who can intrinsically validate biting as a glorious activity.

And the sooner we lessen the extraneous barking, the quieter things will become, and with quiet comes understanding and a great deal less biting.

Song: "Fight the Good Fight" by Triumph

Wine: Hullabaloo Old Vine Zinfandel

Cheese: Piave Vecchio

Three Point Five

How often do we catch ourselves thinking that life has pushed us to the edge? Ever describe someone as living on the fringe or just plain out of control? There is a value that we carry deep within our psyche that understands these descriptors and leads us directly to enunciate observations without pause.

As humans, we have a built-in desire for order, because with order is the illusion of security and control of our environment. Living with the mantra that everything has a place and that everything should be in its place is how we create a comfort zone that places us at its center.

I am reminded of the sixties TV show *Get Smart*. The storyline revolves around a government agency scripted as

"Control" and its never-ending confrontations with their nemesis "KAOS." Control was administered by a group of bumbling, well-intentioned agents that had absolutely no clue about reality. KAOS was a fabrication dedicated to taking over the world for the sole purpose of instituting chaos as a way of life.

Control and chaos are concepts created by our needs for labeling order and disorder. By creating an artificial environment removed from our internal truth, we attempt to deal with these issues outside of ourselves. By giving life to these entities created by our imagination, we empower them to dictate how we would deal with the world around us. These two constructs close our internal guidance system and force us (by our own choosing) to engage on a false battlefield foreign to our heart.

Ironically, in creating the existence of control and chaos, we cede the ability to have any control as we prepare a field fertile for the perpetuation of chaos. We create an oppression of our spirit by giving life to these illusions.

Since we have unleashed these continuous reruns of a sixties sitcom in our lives and have given it free rein to grow with no checks, how do we push the syndication off button?

Actually, the answer is simple. In my world, I have named it three point five. The activation of this mechanism requires only two items. The first is a place where you can pace seven steps, and the second is to believe.

To begin, stand comfortably, close your two eyes, and quiet your mind. There is no need to go "all meditative," because you might fall over, or maybe you just need a quick fix before your next appointment. Silently step forward with your left foot, because this symbolizes leading with your heart, and the energy you want to feel with your first pace is in your heart chakra.

With an equal and measured stride, cover seven steps. Stop and then turn 180 degrees. Lead with your right foot, as this is your tie to Mother Earth, and this will allow her energy to flow through your root chakra to your sacral and then to your solar plexus. Step exactly three point five times.

Turn 90 degrees and stand comfortably. Hold out your arms level with your chest with your left hand palm up to the Creator so He can feed your heart, and your right palm down to Mother Earth so She can give centering and balance.

Quietly allow the energy to flow through. Maybe all you needed was a little bit of calming or maybe a bit of guidance and inspiration. All that truly matters is that you have nurtured your internal energy centers and have prayed comfort. The seven steps is an acknowledgement of the seven chakras; three point five is a prayer for balance; traversing north and south, and then aligning east and west with one palm up and one down recognizes the four directions and invokes the acceptance of "as above, so below."

(Technically there is no need to get a compass for determining your trek. What matters is that you have acknowledged the four directions.)

Three point five is about you and your relationship to the sacred earth that surrounds you and the Creator who gives comfort and love. Being grounded gives the foundation of tranquility in the surreal and illusory world of chaos and control.

Sometimes simple is the best path to walk.

Song: "Take a Giant Step" by Taj Mahal

Wine: Liolo Sonoma Chardonnay

Cheese: Blueberry Stilton

Irreverent Truth of Life

Number 6

If You Think You Are Special, Then You Aren't

Seems a little harsh. As little children, our parental units, aunts, uncles, and other big people in our tiny scope reinforced the notion that we are "special." If you have bought into that notion as your own sentience and independence developed, you have crafted a full-time program of self-deception and ego inflation.

It is true that we are unique. Each of us has gifts, knowledge, and a personality that make every one of us one of a kind. Within our personal world of miraculous individuality, we can bring forth and build on our foundation of singularity.

To be complimented on being special is a sweet notion. Attracting attention to an activity solely for the sake of positive acknowledgement is the height of self-indulgent egoism that debases the essence of the giver(s) of the kudo.

Think about certain folks that regale us with their fantastic accomplishments, given entirely from their selfless sense of public duty, with the intent that we as a collective bestow the moniker of "special" on the person.

Seriously, does this kowtowing activity speak to heart or to ego? And the more we mire ourselves in this debasing ritual, the more we succumb to the effects of surreal symbolism over truthful substance.

Please note, I have not postulated that no one is special. What I have said is that the self-bestowal of that honorarium is self-deception. And now for the big question: can anyone be special?

The answer is absolutely; anyone can be special. And yes, that means anyone. The roadmap begins with the simple concept that *I am third.*

Minimizing ego is the first step in becoming special. Second is expanding your horizons through knowledge and living with your eyes open, and third is allowing your heart to become a coleader of your path.

An easy gauge on the first step is to determine if your activities are for accolades or for the sense of accomplishment. Setting aside ego entirely is not a suggested activity. A healthy dose of ego gives a sense of confidence. Confidence is fed from within; self-importance is fed from without.

Reading, learning, and careful listening cultivate a broader foundation. Even ideas that are anathema to your very being can teach. Blinders work well when total focus is needed, but they create trip hazards (born from ego and arrogance) that never allow you to start your journey.

Coleading with your heart is a sensible approach to mixing empirical and rational cognitive thought with emotion and love. Giving one approach a superior position over the other is like trying to walk with one leg. Again, you will fall flat.

Okay, we have listed the mechanics and methodology of reasoning our way to becoming special. Implementing the concept of *I am third* is the interesting part. It's tough to understand that your purpose is to live in the light and love of your Creator, where your heart and mind must meet and meld as one. It is much easier to accept this ideal of existence as a truth. Then, with that acceptance, the experience of knowledge becomes part of your essence. It's kind of like going home for the first time since you were born.

To love others and to forgive as Christ taught is really tough. As a human, perfect in our own mind, we can be quick to point out other humans' failings. Stepping out of that equation into an understanding of love and equanimity could challenge a saint's patience. And not too many of us are saints.

Living as one who serves the Creator and as one who cares for others places you on the third rung. By definition, you have divested yourself of an interest in self, and you have begun to look to others with love and compassion.

It will be *others* who will look upon you as someone "special." Curiously, the journey to become someone special becomes the instrument that will cause you to have little self-satisfaction or interest in achieving the honest attribute of "special." Gifts given without attachment have no strings.

In short, if everyone is special, no one is special. Accomplishment as well as the pursuit of excellence are worthy endeavors and certainly should be acclaimed for what they are. If little Timmy gets a gold star for winning the spelling bee or some athlete scores the winning touchdown, understand these things for what they are.

Neither of these two activities resides exclusively in one domain or the other at all times. Teach little Timmy the difference between learning for the love of knowledge and the competitive desire to be the best. If the athlete doesn't already grok (you may need to Google this word) the differences between the power of individual accomplishment and the selflessness of giving to his teammates, then hold him with love and help him to open his eyes.

This isn't to say that individual goals and a competitive nature are undesirable attributes. There is a sliding continuum between the points of ego driven self and ethereal altruism. Developing a cognitive mind-set that objectively acknowledges these two points empowers the individual to work at his own betterment as he contributes in a meaningful way to those around him.

Words mean things. Learning to be careful with their meanings and intent gives us a better understanding of this three-dimensional reality. Let's treat each word and phrase as unique, for that is what they are. Allowing trite applications of words to who we are diminishes us and holds us hostage in a cell of our own making.

Song: "Pride of Man" by Quicksilver Messenger Service

Wine: Spellbound Petite Syrah

Cheese: Canadian Black Diamond Cheddar

I Choose Not to Participate

George Washington once spoke about the pitfalls of entangling alliances. I guess he was trying to say that we need to maintain our own space and independence. These alliances can be with other folks, and they can also exist within your own psyche.

Let's start with other folks. Moms and dads know all to well how hard it is to say no and actually stick to it. Whether the child is five or twenty-five, it's easy to give in to his or her wishes. When you break down how the pieces fit together between parent and child, the essence is that you are being moved by the child into participating in whatever the child wants. Your acquiescence to gain a moment of peace or to perceive yourself as accepted is buying into a drama that is of your making.

Using a little bit of common sense allows us to differentiate between legitimate needs for sustenance and love versus "if you don't buy me a candy bar (or a new car), my whole world will end and it will be your fault."

Choosing not to participate in an entangling alliance requires discipline. There are a great many lunatics and salacious, malevolent gossipers who wish to tie you to their wagon. By participating in someone else's muck, you validate their bad behavior, and soon there is no escape. Once escape becomes impossible, misery sets in because your participation becomes a weight that can't be easily jettisoned.

The idea here is not to build a persona of total aloofness, but to find a way to stay above the fray and chaos while maintaining some degree of sanity.

Okay, we have covered the world looking out. Turn your eyes inward, and see the treasure trove of negativity and perceived shortcomings. Everyone does have a handicap or two here and there, but choosing not to participate in their poison can dissipate the vast majority of internal demons that want your attention and participation.

Some folks refer to internal entanglements as hang-ups. A hang-up is defined as an inability to move. You are stuck, swirling in thoughts of inadequacy. Stand back and choose not to participate in the hang-up.

When you run your personal inventory (number 13), some mighty interesting discoveries can be made. When you separate wheat from chaff and then discarding the chaff (number 12), you find things in which you wish to participate.

Let's go deeper on the subject of participation. We all have pains, both physical and heartfelt. Marcus Aurelius was quite the pragmatic stoic, and he acknowledged that there are just some things that can't be addressed with a reorganization of attitude.

Choosing not to participate in physical or emotional pain doesn't mean attempting to ignore your arthritis or your loss of a dear heart. Grant yourself the latitude to effectively deal with hurts in a way that gives control to your spirit. There is strength and understanding in learning how to dominate sufferings that attempt to own you. This isn't easy, but the moment you become subjugated by an internal force is the moment you surrender your free will.

Choosing not to participate is a cognitive skill that can become a reflex when difficult situations arise. Allowing yourself to be mired in "entangling alliances"—with people, with situations, or within yourself—removes your ability to think rationally and to react positively and for the greater good.

No one is going to be in perfect condition on every occasion. Some of us have pains that never cease, family relations that can be too much to bear, or a sadness that seems to never leave. Playing hurt is just one of those things we must do. The alternative is to sit on the bench and eventually turn to stone.

Choose not to participate in the hurts that we all have to some degree or another; choose to participate in the things that heal, that lead to tranquility and, eventually, self-made peace.

Song: "Isn't It a Pity" by George Harrison

Wine: Ranga Ranga Sauvignon Blanc

Cheese: Castello Blue

Irreverent Truth of Life

Number 8

It's Just Going to Take
a Little While

Patience. There has never been a word that causes more exasperation when suggested as a behavior modification to a person in a state of extreme agitation. If anything, the result is quite the opposite. And have you noticed that those who offer such advice rarely accept it themselves when the occasion calls for patience?

We can laugh at this because we have all been on both sides of the coin. Then, if we are honest with ourselves, we sadly think that attempting to summon patience when needed rarely results in a successful conjuring.

Simple things tell us how pressure can build. A boiling teakettle or a bladder after too many beers calls for immediate attention, lest some undesired spillage will occur. Calmly we reach to turn down the burner or we meander off to the restroom without much thought. A situation that needed remedy presented itself, and we addressed it without much thought.

The many adages that have sprung from the well of impatience should serve as checkpoints instead of future lamentations because they were not applied at the right moment. One of my favorites is, "It is easier to do it right the first time." What brilliance! What an aggravation to think back on a project for which I attempted a shortcut, just to have to revisit the failure so I could do it right the *second* time.

Tolerance seems to be the lubricant for the employment of patience. Tolerance is a cognitive activity that calms our attitude but also allows us to see the issue at hand more clearly. Reducing the pressure of the moment is the key that opens our minds to see solutions that were not apparent before, and it gives us the freedom to make better decisions. Remember, if you put yourself in a corner, the only thing you can see and relate to is the corner.

Perspective helps to reduce the anxiety of unknown situations. Developing an overview of whatever circumstance is staring at you can minimize its stature. Whether it is fixing a plugged drain under the sink or some incredibly huge, life-changing activity, develop a plan. Just the act of penning an outline can bring things into focus and put you in control of the whistling teapot.

Building a tolerance for your own frailties or your inability to control something beyond your ken reinforces the notion that you do not have to let the conditions dictate your reaction. With dedication to the idea that you are the architect of your life, you can resume the position of driver as opposed to being a passenger in some horror flick of your own making.

So what if something is going to take a little while? Neil Armstrong had less than sixty seconds of fuel to land Apollo 11 when it became obvious that the intended landing site was not suitable. Mission Control was out of control in that dire situation. Neil told Mission Control it was just going to take a little bit to find the right spot. Neil was patient; he knew the lunar landscape in that landing zone and was tolerant that the condition of having less than sixty seconds to live would not dictate a panicked response, despite the lunacy of those back on Earth. He and Buzz Aldrin landed safely with fifteen seconds of fuel remaining. How beautifully ironic that the landing site was named Tranquility Base.

Things happen that you can't fix, and things happen for which you did not plan but which can be fixed. Courage is defined as engaging either of these circumstances with conviction that neither instance will own you. Wisdom is defined as empirically and objectively categorizing these two items for what they are. Living is defined as dealing effectively with both situations for what they are and then moving on to the next moment of life. The lessons will stay with you, and any pallor of pain or frustration will be relegated to the rearview mirror.

What a rewarding experience to accomplish a task! Even more rewarding is to have navigated through difficult terrain with minimal fuss and a feeling of control by having been patient when challenges were presented. These successes build on themselves. It is never too late to teach patience to yourself or to serve as an example of self-tolerance to another.

So the next time someone counsels patience, push the STOP button. It's okay to take time to step back, breathe, and look around. It is kind of funny how, when removing yourself from the problem, that activity results in you becoming the solution.

Song: "Fifth Dimension" by The Byrds

Wine: Pulenta La Flor Malbec Rose

Cheese: Fontina d'Aosta

Irreverent Truth of Life

Number 9

LMAO, *and You Should Too*

Perhaps the most ecclesiastic activity in which we can engage is to laugh. In case you were not paying attention at the dawn of creation, our Creator is a comedian playing to an audience that is afraid to laugh. Kudos to Voltaire for that keen insight.

We are going to spend a little time on the funny side of life. And quite frankly, visiting the unfunny side of life is akin to a journey into a hell best described by Dante. However, the nature of the beast upon which we ride requires a certain amount of time traipsing around those loathsome nine levels. But that doesn't mean we have to live there and hence be consumed by it.

It is better to pull back to the oasis of understanding that life is an adventure to be enjoyed. Why wear a serious demeanor for all your time here? You won't make it out alive, no matter how pious you act.

In the world of frustration, angst, worry, and physical and emotional pain, there is a sense of being in a deep pool with no handholds or ladder. We can express optimism even though we are being consumed by misery. At this level, the sad truth is that lying to ourselves only results in madness.

Certainly there are those who wish to labor in a mine deep within the bowels of suffering because that is where their solace lies. It can be a fearful act to divorce yourself from the comfort of a realm with which you are familiar. How often have we seen people work diligently to make bad decisions, suffer the consequences, and then make an immediate return to the vending machine that dispenses sorrow and failure? How hard it must be to shake that yoke of serfdom, to repent, and to cross that line into light and laughter.

Reason is found in the halls of the ebullient and gregarious. Judgment is the tool of the condemned who labor in the dark. By definition, a light heart is more open to ideas, and the mind is more enthused with finding

finding employment for engaging prospects. It is so much easier to say yes with a smile on your lips than to attempt a positive rejoinder with a frown upon your person.

What activity gives way to progress more than confidence? Is it not a ubiquitous truth that doubt is a self-fulfilling prophecy? When these two queries are compared, it is quite easy to see which emanated from which school of life.

There is a commitment we make every day with virtually everything we do. To live on the side of LMAO is not adopting the antics of a jester, and to suggest so is foolish. To be positive, to smile, to have a kind word, to hold a door open, or just to engage as a pleasant human being are character traits of a balanced and comfortable person who is willing to give.

As nature moves us through her caresses, we learn that we are all full of weaknesses, and that our foundation is built on looking for strengths. Searching for and then honestly confronting our own weaknesses is an exercise in foundation enhancement. Love for others grows as ego-driven self-love devolves into a distant chamber for an eternal slumber.

A clear mind and light heart are the two requisites for engaging the absurdities that surround us. We learn to reason with those who have no capacity for reason; we learn to speak with those who are confused and entrenched; and we learn to participate in the arena of ideas by persuading hearts and minds. There is a great deal to be said for those who shed light on darkness without passing judgment on what they find.

When we spend time with folks who are trapped on the other side, the best thing we can do is live the example we wish to share. Many will tear at something they don't understand, and they will attempt to destroy it. Don't change to accommodate someone else's misperceptions, because that only confuses the message of laughter and peace. The instant you deviate from what you know is true is the moment you surrender your faith.

Is life so demeaning that we turn from the elixir of life that we have known since infancy? Few things in our human experience are more pleasing than eliciting a coo from a baby. This delight speaks directly to our inner self with a validation that pure joy does exist, and we spend a voyeuristic moment basking in that aura of infant regeneration. Just because we gain years and burdens does not mean we have to surrender our ability to coo. It's still there, and it lives on the side of the mirror that allows laughter and joy.

We have choices and we have free will. Beyond the world of rights and wrongs is a field where imposed afflictions do not exist. I hope to see you there soon!

Song: "Sunlight" by Jesse Colin Young

Wine: Erath Pinot Noir

Cheese: Goat Cheese (chevre)

Eyes Work Only When They Are Open

What a many-faceted blessing to wake each morning—for the fact not only that we are still on the green side of the grass, but also that one of the lovely gifts many of us have is drinking in our surroundings. Things probably haven't changed much during our slumbers. Upon rising we continue to express a sad arrogance in our banal engagement with the wonders of each delight waiting for us.

Our first task in this treatise is to understand that eyes are our contact patch with the world. Imagine the world going by in slow motion and that you have been given the time to explore each and every item in your bedroom before your feet touch the ground.

Focus begins with intent: Aha! Over there is a book I have thought about reading. I will pick it up on the way to making coffee. On the wall by the dresser is a picture of a wolf. Maybe I should think about the things I can teach and learn today. Isn't it fantastic the way the early morning light dispels shadows and gives definition to everything? Might be a lesson in that thought.

What a fantastic habit to make part of your early morning ritual! No longer do you see the world as a separate canvas from your mind, but it becomes something with which to interact meaningfully. Each step becomes a contemplation on beauty, and each journey becomes a treasury of visual gifts.

Now that we have engaged our eyes on the esoteric joys that surround us, it is time to take that second step. On a daily basis we are inundated by information. We are told, "Do this," Don't do that," "These are the facts," and "This is what you should believe."

Remember that our first lesson in opening our eyes was to look at everything and allow each color, fabric, light, article, or event to speak to us in our capacity as an individual. Our second step in learning how to open our eyes builds on the first.

Without question, we are masters of our view. We have the free will to interpret the unfolding landscape for ourselves. If we choose to let another direct our footsteps based on his or her vision, we have abdicated our God-given gift of sight.

In our first step we learned how to appreciate a flower entirely on its own and then build on that to see the plant that supports it, the ground that nurtures it, the bees that pollinate it, and the sunlight and all the surroundings that brought forth such wonderment.

Our second step is a bit braver because we must begin to look for things that are not readily apparent and learn how the pieces fit together. We have learned how to see; now we must learn how to look. We know how the garden fits together with all of its pieces that create life and beauty. We now will learn how to open our eyes more fully to see the pieces of life in their true context and not some preordained path that we must follow in order to be accepted as part of the sightless pack.

How enchanting it has become to be a member of the free-seeing world. We have moved from spectator to engaged participant in the three-dimensional world around us. The third step in learning how to open our eyes is by closing them … and allowing our third eye to open.

Expanding your conscious universe through meditation is your personal tie to the knowledge that comes from within. Relaxing and allowing the world to flow around you begins the process, giving intuition and heightened perception a fertile meadow in which to blossom.

To be quiet is to be with God. In silence we become open to receiving sight that is unavailable to three-dimensional existence. As it was when we first opened our eyes and gained a love and understanding for the little things around us, so it is with our foray into a spiritual relationship with the multidimensional universe that surrounds us.

What new treasures! We have found the ability to walk as individuals in our daily lives guided by seeing and looking, and now we are learning how vision will move us on a path of knowing.

Truly, it is a magnificent blessing living with our eyes open.

Song: "Eyes of the World" by The Grateful Dead

Wine: Hedges CMS Red

Cheese: Piave Vecchio

Coincidence? I Don't Think So

W hat a delightful moment when the phone rings and it's just the person you were thinking about and wished to visit with? Or a dream that prepares us for what would ordinarily be an unexpected and challenging encounter?

So much theory has been promulgated regarding quantum mechanics or string theory. Great minds, both secular and spiritual, have attempted to explain connectivity and the concepts of a matrix or nonlinear time web that surrounds all beings.

I like stories that celebrate the beauty of coincidence that is, indeed, not a coincidence. My favorite illustration of

Irreverent Truth number 11 begins with violence, pain, and fear.

Sarah and Charlie live in our neighborhood. Charlie is retired and gives a lot of his time helping others at the food bank. Sarah is a gifted healer and has never accepted a dime for her compassion and prayers.

Charlie's day always starts early—up with the dogs at first light so both Charlie and his companions can get a bit of exercise. Sarah is left so she can wake slowly on her own terms.

Enter the bad guy. Malicious and evil intent on two legs describes the intruder. Charlie is with the dogs on a walk, and the bad guy knows this. He breaks in and violently attacks Sarah. Beaten and bloodied, Sarah prays for rescue. At that very moment, Charlie bursts into the home and takes on the attacker, many years his junior.

Charlie wrestles the bad guy to the floor and attempts to take the pistol away from the intruder. In the process, Charlie is pummeled by the weapon in the head and body. Charlie gallantly continues the fight until the bad guy decides to quit the scene and run away.

Later that morning at the hospital, Sarah is released to our care. However, Charlie has complications from a cerebral hemorrhage and must be transferred to a facility

75 miles away in Flagstaff specializing in that type of trauma.

Not only is the morning shattered for all concerned, but also two lives of tranquility and giving are forever scarred. And most tragically, our hero lies in a bed far away in an intensive care unit with a most uncertain fate.

Such a beautiful and loving couple are Sarah and Charlie. It is a delightfully quiet and neighborly street on which they lived. What an immediate and horrific impact a wanton act of violence had on their lives.

We gather Sarah up from the hospital and speed to the special place of care to which Charlie has been sent. Sarah is weak and can only think of being with Charlie.

Charlie is resting comfortably upon our arrival at the special care unit. By late that evening, he is talking and the prognosis is very good for a speedy recovery.

On the way back to the Village, Sarah melts into herself and finds comfort in talking about fresh sweet corn covered in butter. She reminisces about wonderful meals she prepared for her children; freshly harvested sweet corn was the centerpiece of so many happy dinners. Her self-comforting continued with her reminiscing about going to the local farmer's market with Charlie and picking the best corn for their table.

There are times we retreat to a safe place in our minds and our hearts when there is just too much hurt to process cognitively or emotionally. Sarah's safe place was memories of family and fresh sweet corn with butter.

It is late when we return to the Village, and the only restaurant open is Roberto's. We slide in just moments before closing time. Dinner is ordered, and we all anticipate the enchiladas that will soon be served.

Immediately prior to our main course arriving, Roberto brings three ears of deliciously fresh, buttered corn to our table. Roberto does not have corn on the menu and has never, ever served corn. No other table in the busy restaurant has been gifted with this special and unsolicited treat.

We were singled out for this special treat not because Roberto knew of the ordeal Sarah had been through. Nor did he have any idea how much she loved fresh corn. Some folks would describe this as a fantastic coincidence. *I don't think so.* Our Creator wished to give Sarah a message, and He tapped Roberto to serve as His angel.

How and why do these special instances occur? It is pretty much a rhetorical question that bubbles forth with anecdotes, both small and large. Sarah will carry with her the certain knowledge that on such a hurtful day, her tears were felt and comforting hands reached to hold her securely in His heart.

Song: "Angel" by Jimi Hendrix

Wine: Guarchi Sonoma Pinot Noirr

Cheese: Parmigano-Reggiano

Irreverent Truth of Life

Number 12

Take Out the Garbage

G arbage can best be thought of as something that was once in your life, but for some reason or other, you no longer have any use for it. One of the most curious behaviors humans engage in is the accumulation of garbage. Some dispose of the offending rubbish quickly, and others choose to allow the garbage to become a monument unto itself.

The real trick is to identify just exactly what garbage is. After all, deciding what people or situations require the old heave-ho can have quite a bit of emotion attached to it.

Hurtful lovers, abusive relationships, parasitic "friends," and nasty people at work are pretty easy to label as human debris that should be jettisoned. When crafting a list to take curbside, be sure to include anyone or any situation that rises to the level of garbage.

Now that you have that long list ready and you are feeling empowered because you are going to show those bums just who is in charge, it's time to calm down. To have worked yourself up to a state of agitation that requires the act of dismissing people and things, you have allowed all of those people and things to live in your head rent-free. Maybe the problem is not entirely with your lover or with that cretin landlord who won't fix the leaky faucet.

You invited all of those people and situations into your life, and it's quite true that you can dismiss them at any time you choose. It's really simple. All you have to do is gather all of the offending party's stuff, and out to the street it goes. Problem solved, right?

Someone else's stuff may be tossed out on the rubbish heap, but then you haven't evicted the essence of the problem. To really get a handle on what needs to be tossed, you need to identify what precipitated the pile of garbage to accumulate in the first place.

Perhaps the best place to start is you. How exactly is it that you attract bad landlords or nasty coworkers or bad lovers or angry clerks at the grocery store? All these conditions are garbage and should be discarded.

There are times when some ugly circumstance presents itself and you have the good sense just to walk away. And you congratulate yourself that the garbage never even got close to sticking to you. Hooray!

Then, perhaps, to gain a better perspective on the garbage in your life, a closer look at how you invited the garbage into your life is in order. After careful consideration, you may come to the conclusion that your occupation will always put you in contact with folks with whom you will never get along with. You will never see the Dali Lama and Simon Cowell on tour together.

Your significant other doesn't work, and this is you third relationship with an unemployed sponge. This bad turn of events is not his or her fault. You are the magnet that allowed the universe to deposit another freeloader in your life.

Why don't you check landlords for their BBB ratings before renting? The leaky faucet and bad landlord belong to you, because that is what you wanted.

The trick is to identify the garbage. The solution is to understand why it accumulates in your life. Maybe you had nothing to do with the grief on your doorstep. But you have to honestly make that assessment first.

Can things start out great and later turn to rubbish? You bet they can. Identify the garbage and honestly assess why it became garbage. It just may be the type of garbage that isn't garbage, and all it needs is a proper washing and loving attention.

It is so easy, and gutless, to lay the blame somewhere else and immediately toss the offending item. The hard thing is to understand why a particular piece of waste material has crossed your path. And the even harder thing still is to learn the lesson it has to teach and give thanks that a gift experience has been granted you.

Song: "Take It Back" by Cream

Wine: Spring Valley Nina Lee

Cheese: Muenster

Irreverent Truth of Life

Number 13

Inventory Yourself

N ow, this can get a bit personal and disconcerting. The intent here is not to allow you to dwell on missed opportunities at self-betterment, but rather to do the brutally honest task of self-assessment by inventorying your skills, education, and experiences.

Our first day on this planet is the moment we begin building our personal inventory. Snuggle up close to Mom and we are warm, take a breast and our bellies become full and we sleep. Pretty good for the first day. Our instincts directed us immediately on the path to understanding the meaning of life, sustenance, and unconditional love.

Every day from that point on, we garner experience through stimuli, both wanted and unwanted. Chocolate cake tastes great, and a hot stove burns. Pretty simple stuff, but the train keeps rolling. Soon we learn to walk, read, and communicate.

Nothing is cast in stone, and how we individually build our own repertoire of experiences is entirely up to each person. Some folks have a harder time because of disabilities, poverty, a difficult home life, or just non-engagement. Non-engagement can be born of laziness or just plain not having any interest in moving your own ball further down the field.

For the most part, those of us who choose to build an inventory early in life tend to be more successful materially and/or spiritually. Those who choose not to craft anything of substance on their personal foundation tend to blame others for their shortcomings.

Everyone can relate to acquiring knowledge through education. Books, mentors, and classrooms create a structure that fills an individual with classic personal empowerment. Engineering, architecture, medicine, law, and the like are taught in a very structured environment. Your level of cerebral engagement will determine just how well you fill your reservoir.

If you work diligently at doing "just enough to get by," your abilities to excel become limited. Placing self-imposed boundaries on yourself short changes the gift of infinite capacity granted so many of us.

There is another pool of inventory to fill, and it relates to the esoteric. Building an appreciation of beauty is not an adult activity. Rather, the sensitivity of innocence and first-day consciousness begins this filing cabinet. Certainly there is a great deal to learn about different art forms and attaching definitions to different genres. However, the basic building block of wide-eyed wonder and heart-felt emotion is the elementary fountain that nourishes a graduated appreciation of beauty in all its forms. Remembering this touchstone of innocent reverence removes inhibitions and preconceived notions.

Finally, we get to the story time of this chapter. A grandfather and grandson sit under a moonlit sky as they watch the embers of the fire slowly pass away. "Grandfather, I have a question," states the grandson. "There are times I am angry with my friends, and then there are times I am happy with my friends. Why?"

"Grandson, think of two wolves that live within you. One is evil, jealousy, hate, and hurt. The other is good, charity, love, and forgiveness. They will always battle one another."

"If they are always fighting each other, then one must win, right, Grandfather? How do I know which one wins?"

"The one you feed."

Nearly everyone has heard this tale, but the point the grandfather is making is that within each of us we carry an inventory of characteristics, and it is our choice as to which trait we wish to apply at any given moment.

One last item: Old People. By definition, old people carry more inventory than young people. It is our ancestors who explored continents and the stars. Their writings are important because they add to our experiences without each of us having to reinvent the wheel.

Our present-day elders are the ones who gave us moon walks, fantastic medical healings, cell phones, and so much more. Perhaps we should spend more time listening with respect to those who have just gone before us, not only for the sake of building inventory, but because we too will have gifts to hand down.

Looking at your personal inventory will begin as a linear and concrete pursuit. As your journey of introspection carries on, you will begin to dig out abstract ideas and begin to give them definition—not so much to domesticate and categorize the amorphous parts of your inventory, but to name them, understand them, and build upon them.

Song: "Who Are You?" by The Who

Wine: Klinker Brick Old Vine Zinfandel

Cheese: Maytag Blue

Irreverent Truth of Life

Number 14

An Infinite Number of Monkeys

Sooner or later, so goes the theorem, an infinite number of monkeys with an infinite number of typewriters with an infinity of time could eventually type Shakespeare's works. It is a statistical probability of a gazillion to one, but it is a probability nonetheless. I define this as accidental brilliance, and by the laws of the universe, there is a place for it.

One of the beautiful gifts the Creator gave us is sentience. What a delightful position to be in to contemplate the concept of "I AM." Our information download begins with our first breath, and soon enough Mom and Dad get to hear their darling two-year-old enunciate in a shrill voice, *"Mine!"* Yep, that is really the first step in acknowledging that we are an individual and capable of possession.

Time goes by, and we begin to be shaped and packaged into the rituals and expectations of the society, culture, and laws prevalent in the little dome we call life. We are educated, praised, cajoled, punished, rewarded, and squeezed into a mold that opens only on one end. Attempting to look beyond that cubicle is just not encouraged.

From the dawn of human civilization (now there's an oxymoron), there has been an enlightened class of chattering beings. Their deafening chorus is much like an infinite number of monkeys hammering on typewriters. On a very rare occasion, something positively brilliant shines through. And as we have learned, that is to be expected, statistically speaking. Our job is to separate the mountains of chaff from the kernels of wheat.

Along with the gift of sentience, we have free will. Together they can be a potent combination. Stifle either one, and the other withers to a sad state of missed promise. How can you build a dream if you are hollow and live in a rut?

We face three big questions: How do we get our arms around the concept of sentience? Where does free will begin, and where do convention and conformity end? And finally, out of the infinite number of gibberish-chattering monkeys, how do we find the one that speaks truth?

Let's start at the beginning, which is always a good place to start, and pick up the pieces of our identity. Objectively, without attaching any labels of good or bad and attempting to assign blame or pass judgment, look at your point of inception. Think about your parents and the environment into which you were born. This is a form of personal analysis, and there is no place for subjective opinions. There are a lot of things that require passion and emotion, but this internal assessment is not one of them.

Go through your formative years and follow yourself to this present moment. Spend some time on the concept of "I AM" as it relates to you. About this time, you should begin to develop an appreciation for the beautiful instrument of creation that you are. Throw in a little warm fuzzy feeling, and you begin to feel love. Your memories start to fill in the little bits and pieces of your being, honoring a self-induced understanding that indeed "I AM."

Wow, now we have to get a handle on free will. From day one we were subjected to overlords impinging on our creative abilities. It may be a little rough calling Mom and Dad overlords with their love and benevolent dictatorship.

If our parental units hadn't placed limitations on us, we probably would not have lived long enough to blame our future hang-ups on them. Society and culture have had quite a hand in melding us into useful squares pegs as well.

Exercising free will is a process of thought resulting in action. I once saw a refrigerator magnet emblazoned in Comic Sans: "The Best Way to Predict the Future Is to Invent It." I bought it and have it displayed prominently in my office, because I believe that is the essence of free will. To believe you can effect a change either through deed or thought is to acknowledge that you exist as an individual and that you can cast off convention and think beyond your assigned cubicle. A determined individual is one who is open to the concept of free will.

Like minds attract one another. There is no need to climb to the mountaintop and seek the guru. Eventually your paths will cross, and you will both know that you are kindred spirits that have shunned the chattering class.

Excellence and exceptionalism are traits earned by those who believe in themselves, have accepted themselves for who they are, and have actively chosen to think for themselves. By definition, not everyone will awaken. It requires self-examination, discipline, and leaving the comfort zone of a well-ordered cubicle. But then again, there is no greater joy of clarity we can experience than leaving a reality that accepts monkeys as the wisdom keepers.

Song: "Stranger in a Strange Land" by Leon Russell

Wine: Vignetti del Sole Pinot Grigio

Cheese: Taleggio

Poetry, Songs, and Butterflies

Poetry, songs, and butterflies are candy for the eyes, ears, and mind. They feed the spirit of our being. And the delightful thing about these sweets is there is not a calorie to be found!

Poetry, for my purpose here, comprises all written and spoken language. How divine to be able to communicate a thought from one being to another! And even more amazing is the sentient activity that crafted thought and turned it into a moment of beauty and sharing.

To convey thought with artistry is such a gift. Whether we are wrapped up in the nuances of the fantastic Scripture or Shakespeare or a love letter from home, our hearts are touched and images take shape in our minds.

Words mean things, and their purpose is to give life to ideas, invoke emotions, and emanate expression. We speak (or write) to educate, to document, to persuade, or for our own pleasure. We also use words to denigrate, tear at, or intentionally deceive one another.

The skills we employ in the realm of wordsmithing tell the receiver how concerned we are about thoughtfully and completely sharing our message. Underutilizing the tools we have at hand serves no one and stands on its own as a disgraceful disregard for the gift of communication.

Not everyone is a Hemmingway or William Jennings Bryan, but we all have the access to the toolbox of expression. To make an effort in this arena honors not only the receiver, but also those who have toiled in the past to make communication fun and effective.

Read the old texts of artistic prose and parody. Adopt some of the ways of the old authors as your own. Their spirits will love you. With these seeds of prior brilliance, your own mannerisms will mature, and the joyous moment of truly sharing your privately crafted thoughts will be wholly revealed. To steal from one is plagiarism; to steal from many is research. So, go and enjoy the research. It will be a well-lit and fun pursuit.

Songs are composed of melodies and words. Sometimes they get stuck in your head and just won't leave. They make you laugh, cry, sing along, dance, and wish you could play a guitar too. There are radios, stereos, eight-tracks, iPods, concerts, street-corner musicians, and a whole host of other devices and venues that attract us like small pebbles to the inside of open-toed sandals. What is it that ignites our attention and feeds our appetite in a way that causes us to lust for more?

We all have a favorite song. Many couples have a song they believe was written just for them. And there's a song we want played at our funeral party. Music seems to be the consuming expression that speaks to us, describes our loves, or tells others how we lived our life.

There is a visceral connection we have with music that flows freely through us. We have danced a waltz and felt divine, twisted the night away with naught more than happy gyrations, sang (or attempted to sing) like a rock star in a karoke setting, or just allowed the background sounds to fill our days.

There is a tie running from our fundamental nature to the tunes we funnel through our ears into our entire being. Is it a desire that we be constantly entertained, or is it a source of nourishment for our souls? Kind of a chicken or egg thing, isn't it? I do know that birds sing and that there is rhythm in life, so I am going to default to the position that the gift of song comes from God, and it's a darned good one at that. Amazing how right we got something by listening to the world around us.

Butterflies in my mind equal art—colors, shapes, beauty, and natural purpose, all brought together in perfect harmony. And they float in the air! It doesn't get any more ethereal or transcendent than that. It is no wonder we as humans have looked to the natural world for inspiration in our art. We paint landscapes, portraits, and animals; we carve statues and likenesses; and we create jewelry.

With just about anything we touch, we can find a way to design something beautiful and awe inspiring. It is a direct connection to our higher nature to meld materials into manifestations of beauty. When we spend time in our artistic mode, it becomes difficult to climb off that pony and find reasons to hate.

As a practical matter, engineers who create in a mode of higher awareness, find ways to enrich the human experience by allowing a subconscious sublimation of natural relations to influence and guide his hand.

Trying to describe everything that describes is a bit of a task. The lesson here is to understand that we are masters of our interactions with each other, and all that we do is subject to our essence and our environment. We have the ability to influence the things that influence us, but do we have the wisdom to allow the Creator's love and wonder to flow through our being to create art?

To paraphrase an old English guy, we are infinite in our capacity to reason, but how limited we are to understand it. Maybe the best way to live is to leave limits behind and give way to our natural state of being with poetry, songs, and butterflies. It's kind of ironic how understanding begins when we surrender our desire to understand.

Song: "Across the Universe" by The Beatles

Wine: Tangent Pinot Blanc

Cheese: Baby Swiss

Irreverent Truth of Life

Number 16

Breathing and Kindness Are One in the Same

My dad always signed his letters to my wife and I with the advice, "Be kind to each other." It's a little bit of a quaint thought until you realize it is a statement of being.

As is my wont, I like to break things down by definition and practice. *Kind* is defined as humane, caring, charitable, sympathetic, or understanding. All of these activities require that you set aside your ego or hidden motive and open yourself to another.

"Be kind to each other" was such a simple notion that Dad scripted. But exactly how and when should kindness be expressed? Who should it be reserved for? Why should you let your guard down and trust that someone won't mistake your kindness for weakness to be exploited?

Obviously Dad had a screw loose. Why participate in any activity that doesn't have a benefit for me? Sure, being "kind" to the wife can be fun, and it could yield a few benefits.

There is a trade-off with adopting kindness as a strategy for facing the world and all the people and things in it. Kindness crowds out anger and doesn't allow rage a place to grow. And there seems to be an abundance of patience needed for the slow checker at the grocery store or the mullet who just stole your parking place at the mall. None of that really matters if your default position is kindness.

There aren't too many folks that can hold it together all day every day. There's only one guy that even came close, and as best I can recall, even He had a hissy fit in the temple with some moneychangers.

Perhaps the best way to start on the path to being kind is to do something simple. As cliché as it sounds, just smile. And mean it, damn it!

Insincerity breeds contempt. If you wish to share a small part of your being with another, it should be a genuine reflection of what you wish to give. Think about that reap-what-you-sow adage that has survived countless generations. There must be a reason it's still here.

Don't miss an opportunity to shine in another's heart with your smile. The moment you get a smile in return that is all love, the addiction begins.

Being kind can fall into that realm of being "just what you do." This connotation is not meant to demean the activity of being kind; rather, it enhances the concept. There are no scorecards or agendas allowed in a world of selfless love.

Soon the acts of kindness begin to invade your life—little things like holding a door for someone with her arms full or taking the time to help a lost dog find its mom and dad. Some gestures are fleeting, and others can be lifelong challenges, but they are all acts coming from your heart with no strings attached.

Thoughts of anger or angst can't exist in a head where the heart is open. Curiously, acts of kindness seem to build on one another, and before too long, other folks are choosing to participate. I guess one could say the malady is the cure.

To understand that breathing and kindness are one in the same is to viscerally acknowledge that they are both activities that can be best described as "just what you do." If it were easy, everyone would do it. Being kind is a chosen activity that requires a release of ego and a belief in love of others.

It's funny how our elders use simple words to teach us greater understandings. Yes, Dad was right. We should all be kind to each other.

Song: "Get Together" by The Youngbloods

Wine: Evodia Old Vine Garnacha

Cheese: Havarti

Irreverent Truth of Life

Number 17

A Slapped Cheek Is a Past Event

W ow! To think that such an egregious attack on your person (literally or figuratively) can be relegated to the pile of trifles that never occurred. Well, actually the concept of forgiveness is a bit more complicated than a trite naysaying. There are quite a few moving parts to the process and a prerequisite that one can discern illusion from truth.

By definition, it takes a sender and a receiver for forgiveness to take place. If there is no one willing to accept the forgiveness, the process is known as "letting it go." If you choose to carry a weight around with you, that is your choice.

There is a third position that comes into play regarding a slapped cheek, and that is righteous wrath. A reaction that could result in a return slap to a trespass must first pass a test. Is the perceived transgression something that lives in reality and truthfully needs to be addressed?

Handing out "forgiveness passes" is a form of self-deception and a self-serving practice of whimsical false altruism and egoism. To see through the mountains that aren't there is to understand that every trespass exists in a reality that is not real. This vision separates you from the three-dimensional world and places you in Spirit, and in Spirit there can be no harm done to you.

With tranquility as your foundation, it becomes easier to rise above the actions surrounding you and then to honestly release the instance of slight and subsequently gift the trespasser with love and forgiveness. A calm mind and heart cannot be unsettled into making irrational judgments and poor relations.

With the disassembly of our manufactured walls, we find that there are no pursuers who wish us harm, because there is no harm that can be made against one who is at peace. We can only lay comfort at our own doorstep, and if another is worthy, it should be shared.

When we leave our personal fortress, we can openly ask ourselves what pains we have brought others and whether we are able to forgive ourselves for things we have done to ourselves as well as to others? As long as we are looking in this mirror, ask the reflection if you have unjustly accused another of something you have failed to hold yourself accountable for as well?

To wander through the midnight of an unforgiving mind is to live in fear and paranoia. The haunting despair that lives in your heart becomes bolstered through a false confidence and self-actualization dependent on lies for sustenance. This is a vicious cycle that drives madness and a deception that carries other souls along with it because of its power. Living in a world of denial is easy because every action becomes justified based on the individual's perception of infallibility.

Learning to condemn another is learning to condemn yourself. Justifiable reactions to hurts or pain must take place outside of ego. This isn't to say that allowing others to cause injury is to be condoned as a forgivable sin with no retribution, but rather that any return of injury can only be accomplished without the passion of revenge.

Admitting that the practice of withdrawing from the truth of spiritual essence began when you were a baby and has built itself into a formidable zone of perceived personal comfort is the first step to acquiring the tools to forgive. There is no need for self-immolation, just a quiet acquiescence that there are new lessons to learn and old ways to abandon.

Leave pretense behind. Be free to express yourself in truth, and there will never be a need for an apology.

To learn how to practice the concepts of forgiveness is to live in grace. Gratitude supplants negative emotions of hateful judgment of others and self-loathing. With this calming balance comes perspective and maturity of spirit. Ego takes a secondary position to good sense and relations.

Remembering an act of forgiveness lessens its value. There is no scorecard to keep, because that implies your gift is about you and not the desire for complete dissolution of a past instance. Let the illusions be washed away and a clean slate be prepared. Knowing that truth exists only in Spirit removes your ability to judge and maintain a ledger of transgressions.

Protect your peace with an open heart and open eyes. And never cede your essence to another by willing surrender.

Song: "Heart of the Matter" by Don Henley

Wine: Klinker Brick Farrah Syrah

Cheese: Canadian Cheddar

Irreverent Truth of Life

Number 18

Even When I Was Broke, I Was Rich

Everyone has heard about the Law of Attraction. And there are a lot of folks who have implored the universe to send riches and good health their way. More often than not, the pot of wished-for gold never arrives.

Quite frankly, the universe has very little use for whiners and beggars. Yes, there are those deserving of kindness and love, and my most heartfelt intent is not to disparage those folks. This diatribe is directed at those of us who are whole in our faculties.

Let's go ahead and address the concept of charity. Many of us have needed help and were grateful that our neighbors and our government were there to lend a hand. There was a time in my life when I physically could not provide for myself, and it would have been nearly impossible without help to pick up the pieces and resume a productive life.

Poverty does suck. Been there, done that, but I never participated in the culture of poverty. To be poor is to buy into the idea that an outside force oppresses you and that there is no remedy available for your condition.

I am not advocating the concept that only wealthy people can be happy. The principal in play here is crowding out the negative thought of lack and replacing it with the energy of self-empowerment.

Poor people, by definition, can never be happy, because they have limited their personal abilities to achieve. Centralizing your entire existence around jealousy of another's property combined with the intent to take what is not yours is a classic form of envy decried in the Ten Commandments. Allowing this energy to focus your activities destroys who you are and forces you deeper into the pit of self-loathing. This is a form of self-actualization that encodes within your essence the condition of being poor.

How strange to think that the wealthy banker living in the penthouse could be the poorest man in town.

For my purposes here, I have defined wealth as an accumulation of assets, whether it be cash, cars, or property. To be rich is the condition that does not ascribe to the concept of lack. Wealth is a state of physical accounting. Rich, on the other hand, speaks to a positive review of self and the appointments we make within our own universe to attract success.

These two characteristics are learned. Wealth—and the desire for wealth—is a behavior that is quite base, yet is the most prevalent activity in which we engage. Materialism just comes naturally to humans. As children, we want all the candy bars in the display at the grocery store, and as adults we lust after someone else's new car. It's called wealth envy for a reason, and the majority of our laws and social mores place a limit on just how far we can extend our greedy mitts into our neighbor's pocket.

To be rich is an internal process and discipline. There are things that rich people do that poor people just do not do. A regimented approach to activities and pursuits in life does not guarantee financial success, and in all instances, money and toys are not the endgame.

One of the most difficult conundrums I have ever tried to comprehend is to understand why poor people are poor. Does it have to do with education or desire or just terrible circumstance? To a degree these can all be true. Perhaps the overriding attribute is the fear of being rich. Rich is a condition born of attitude. It requires a certain work ethic and application of self.

There is a built-in unfairness in life, and the nonteaching of how to become rich is one of the most cruel and oppressive lessons visited upon all folks who live on this planet. Once again, rich isn't about money; it is wealth acquisition that is all about the Benjamins.

An old story overheard the other day goes like this. Two well-off guys died at about the same time. Their friends were counting up the assets of the two guys to see who won in life. All of a sudden, they realized that it didn't matter. Both guys were dead. They adjourned the ad hoc frivolity and headed to the bar.

This tale illustrates our incessant obsession with wealth. Had the guys thought about it, the only real accounting is at the Pearly Gates.

The abilities we are given allow us to compete for wealth accumulation. We are also given the gifts to elevate our being and compete within ourselves to be rich. Everybody knows the guy with a double platinum Visa. The relevant question between this guy and his Creator has so much more to do with riches than wealth.

I have been broke more than one time in my life. My car was my home; I have taken baths at the car wash; and a cold can of beans was a real treat. I also have had money. None of those things matter. I was always, and still am, a very rich man.

Number 13 really is a nice tie-in right about now, but that may be for another evening's round of discussion.

Song: "Inside" by Jethro Tull

Wine: Paul Hobbs Beckstoffer Las Piedras Vineyard Cabernet Suvignon

Cheese: Jarlsberg

Irreverent Truth of Life

Number 19

Incomplete

What a worthy goal! To always feel incomplete, to never be sated, to always feel that the brass ring is just one inch away is a condition to be pursued devoutly. There is a difference between an accomplished individual and one who has accomplished all. The illusion of having accomplished all, by definition, is impossible and manifests ego-driven smugness.

There is a certain celestial irony to acquiring knowledge and skills. As we move on the path of life, each stone of positive experience we stop to pick up actually lightens our step. Our mission is to pass by those stones that create a burden, and our prayer for guidance is to know the difference. On occasion, we gather weights that slow our journey. These, too, result in teachable moments, provided we are prepared to learn from them and vow not to harvest another negative rock.

The concept of incomplete is a self-empowering idea that, among other things, promotes curiosity, a thirst for the next book, and a desire to learn. "Eyes work only when they are open" (number 10) is the practice that creates the notion that we have more steps to walk and that each step builds a consciousness that can be quenched only temporarily.

We can equate a moment of gratification with the feeling we have after a good night's sleep. How refreshing it is to awaken to a new dawn and the rituals of preparing for that day's adventures. One night's rest is the energy that moves us forward for the next several hours, and the same can be said for each experience. A single night's sleep doesn't last a lifetime and neither will a prior moment of learning.

To live in the realm of incomplete compels us to always do our individual best. Excellence can be pursued when we are balanced with our environment and with those around us. Conversely, the world around us does not need to be in a simpatico relationship with truth or with our being. We are the ones who must apply the definition of excellence to ourselves and, by extension, allow only excellence to be in our field of vision. If there are challenges, we find solutions. If there is hate, we find love. The quest for positive influences is an attribute of the pursuit of excellence, and this pursuit is a process that never can be completed.

Sharing can be passive or active. Touching another by example or through engagement is an experience of growth for both parties. This isn't to say that one practice is exclusive to itself, but it can exist separately or in some combination.

A particularly poignant example of passive sharing is role models. History is replete with icons of legendary stature: Jesus Christ, Hercules, and George Washington, just to name a few. They lived lives of excellence and shared their essence of being through example. No matter the challenge, they understood that their lives would be complete only on the day they stood before their maker.

One of the finest examples of engaged sharing is Helen Keller's teacher, Anne Sullivan. It would have been easy for Anne to walk away from Helen, but Anne was from the school of excellence and had an innate understanding that the process of sharing the world with a blind and deaf girl would be a commitment that would never end.

Within each of us is a well that can never run dry. If we choose not to draw from it, that's our problem and not the source's inadequacies. We call this elixir love. It can be quite a painful journey to engage ourselves in the task of lowering the bucket into a chasm of faith and hoping it returns full. It can hurt when we look into the freshly retrieved pail only to find it empty.

A field that is never irrigated will lie fallow for eternity. How brave is the gardener to provide the sustenance the field requires, even if no crop ever grows as a reward for his or her tender care? Even braver still is the gardener who reaps only sorrow for his or her efforts, only to try again. How sad for those who choose to never tap their well after one heartache.

It seems counterintuitive to believe that the only way to be whole is to travel knowing that your journey will always be incomplete. The point here is to never yield to negativity, a self-aggrandizing ego, or the idea that there is nothing left to share or to love. Never be less than the best you can be.

Song: Runnin' Down a Dream by Tom Petty

Wine: Antica Napa Chardonnay

Cheese: Parmigano-Reggiano

Irreverent Truth of Life

Number 20

Boy Meets Girl

O r maybe, it's girl meets boy. It doesn't really matter where the lightning comes from, it's just knowing that it does. And it is fantastic when it lights the world for both the boy and the girl!

This little vignette is not advice on love and all the excited little hormones that race through our bodies and cause us to do things that will embarrass our future progeny and cause our parents to blush because their memories of past silliness have been sparked.

Men and women are different. The question is, how did we get to be different? And furthermore, is that a good thing? After all, if we were androgynous or even hermaphrodite, wouldn't that put all the divorce attorneys out of business? How delightful—no interruptions during Sunday afternoon football. Or window shopping for new shoes would become a national pastime for all couples.

Patriarchs build nations, make things out of steel, and father children who will bear their surname. They build an external shell of impenetrable strength and stoic behavior that never waivers and is always confident, no matter how wrong they are.

Women lead with their heart and their womb. Within their world, the home is kept and the children are nurtured so they may be made ready to accept their roles as dictated by society.

Men are strong and women are weak. Men make the decisions that cause the world to go 'round, and women make sure things are dusted and tidy. These are the paradigms that have built cubicles around us and stifle our ability to share thoughts and emotions.

Now that I have your attention, the point I am driving at is that we are different, and both genders have built-in differences that make it almost impossible to communicate. Thank God for animal magnetism, or we would probably never have gotten past the first generation of humans.

Men, take a look at yourselves. The only real touchstone we have for understanding how to share our emotions is that which is encoded in us, which makes us male. It's a little difficult to share your essence with a woman if all you understand is how to communicate in your default, programmed position as male.

Women, the good Lord made you the givers of life as well as the carriers of love and tenderness. This is your language, and it is who you are. Communicating with other women in female-speak is easy. Attempting to share things with a man from your inner being can be more than a challenge.

We both have wonderful traits and a spiritual composite that makes us indispensable to one another. Now, this is where the math gets tricky. What has just been defined is one being known as male and the other as female. Arithmetically we would add one plus one to get two.

Weddings support this notion by pronouncing us as man and wife. One plus one is two. Mr. and Mrs., *et vir & et ux*, for you Latin majors out there. Instead of being united as one in matrimony, we are immediately sent to our respective corners on our honeymoon night.

For some of you, my examples may be a tad extreme, and you feel that they don't fit you. Whatever. We are who we are. I am not telling men to get in touch with their feelings or for the women to become their inner warrior woman.

When boy meets girl, the lightning does strike, and it is fantastic. Men seem more caring and romantic, while the women seem more understanding and forgiving of us as males. As time goes by, many of us begin to retreat into our corners of maleness and femaleness instead of working on expanding that initial shared vocabulary of love and affection.

Shakespeare wrote, "Wisely and slow, they stumble that run fast." I don't think these two thoughts are necessarily exclusive of each other. It is a happy moment to whirl like a dervish in the sun, and such sweetness to never lose that memory by "wisely and slowly" nurturing it into a bloom that only grows brighter.

The delight of a first kiss and ensuing late-night pillow talk is the Rosetta Stone that begins the bridge between men and women. Don't surrender who you are; instead surrender the gate that guards your inner being.

Maybe an afternoon looking at Gucci bags or a tailgate party at Cowboys Stadium isn't such a difficult thing to do. The no-strings-attached willingness to share and participate in the world of another breaks down the language barriers imposed on us by gender, history, and society. Before too long, the old equation itself will be challenged and reconfigured as one plus one does indeed equal one.

Song: "Romeo and Juliet" by Dire Straits

Wine: Flowers Perennial Sonoma Pinot Noir

Cheese: Gorgonzola

Irreverent Truth of Life

Number 21

Figure It Out

I saved this part for last. We have covered everything from the meaning of life to romance. All the tools are in place to help you become an independent thinker.

Independent thinker in grammatical terms is an adjective followed by a noun. In this treatise, they are two different words that can exist together only if you are independent and you are a thinker.

You become part of the gestalt, part of the human equation, part of the esoteric ethereal world that surrounds us by learning to acknowledge the pool called existence and then choosing to swim in it. This does not mean you surrender your individuality, for that should always be held inviolate, but it means your essence is shared and mixed with all that exists.

Learning how to be one with all while maintaining your independence is a cognitive pursuit. It is so easy to allow ourselves to become identified with one group or another because our desire to be accepted outweighs the kernel of truth within us that decries acceptance for the sake of acceptance.

Independence of the individual spirit creates a bit of an aloof demeanor. Within this degree of separation you spend time asking for guidance based upon the things you know to be true. You know it is important to be kind, you know forgiveness is a release, and you know there is a long list of memories, both learned and experienced, that have fabricated the foundation of truth for you.

Spending a moment to reflect is nothing more than checking your hard drive for data and allowing your mind to open so you may receive more information. There are some very beautiful teachings that remind us to quiet ourselves. The irreverent truth number 5 has a few tips on this.

Thinking involves work. Some issues will cross your path, and you may surprise yourself that you have all the information in your personal inventory to craft an answer or action. Congratulate yourself on having applied yourself well in building a warehouse of knowledge.

If you reach for an answer and all the data isn't there, or if there is conflicting information, spend the time to do the research to develop an answer. I know of at least five different ways to bake a potato. I tried all five, and now I know what works best for me. If I had not checked all five, but followed only what my neighbor told me, I would have surrendered my independence, and I would not be able to claim the moniker of thinker. This is a simplistic example, but you can see how it can be extrapolated to bigger questions.

Choosing not to be independent and choosing not to think is just fine. A lot of folks do quite well living a vacuous existence. If you choose to surrender, no one should denigrate your choice. The rest of us who are participating in the real world just ask that you remain on the porch and don't do anything to upset the apple cart of those who are independent thinkers and are engaged in the arena of ideas.

Emotion is not a quantifiable measure of concrete analysis. If you feel something should be a certain way, learn how to explain it. Please don't state that it is mean to leave a dog out in the snow. Most of us get that. Tell us why it is a bad idea. Doing the research engages your cerebral faculties. And when you are tied to a desire to address the issue of snowbound hounds, you will be more persuasive, and your audience will be more willing to give your statement credence.

Obviously a dog stranded in snow is a simplistic scenario. The intent behind irreverent truth 21 is to lay the groundwork on how to "figure it out."

Preconceived notions based on feelings and a minimum of data may strike a cord of agreement with some folks. The idea here is to be prepared if your sacred cow is set to be gored and you have no factual foundation from which to defend Bessie.

To represent Bessie effectively, divest yourself of emotional ties to any preconceived notions. Study the issue, both pros and cons, and then develop your thoughts. This is when the brilliance of empirically based dialectic is able to shine and cascade persuasion on the participants.

It isn't always easy to figure things out. Sometimes we need help from friends, reading materials, spiritual leaders, or even a song on the radio.

If you have read this far into this book, you are a thinker and you enjoy the challenge of presenting and defending your ideas. By this time many of your beliefs may have been augmented or even challenged outright. Congratulations and welcome to the arena of ideas! The water here is warm, and we are always ready for more to join us.

Song: "Forever Young" by Bob Dylan

Wine: Bogle Phantom, blend of Syrah, Zinfandel, and Mourvedre

Cheese: Boar's Head Canadian White Cheddar